Your Special Needs Child

....

Help for Weary Parents

Stephen Viars

New
Growth
Press
www.newgrowthpress.com

New Growth Press, Greensboro, NC 27404
www.newgrowthpress.com
Copyright © 2011 by Stephen Viars.
All rights reserved. Published 2011

Cover Design: Tandem Creative, Tom Temple,
tandemcreative.net

Typesetting: Lisa Parnell, lparnell.com

ISBN-10: 1-936768-45-3
ISBN-13: 978-1-936768-45-5

Library of Congress Cataloging-in-Publication Data
Viars, Stephen, 1960–
  Your special needs child : help for weary parents / Stephen Viars.
    p. cm.
  Includes bibliographical references and index.
  ISBN-13: 978-1-936768-45-5 (alk. paper)
  ISBN-10: 1-936768-45-3 (alk. paper)
 1. Parents of children with disabilities—Religious life.
2. Parenting—Religious aspects—Christianity. 3. Child
rearing—Religious aspects—Christianity. I. Title.
  BV4596.P35V53 2011
  248.8'45—dc23
                                              2011038262

Printed in Canada
20 19 18 17 16 15 14 13   3 4 5 6 7

What is the number-one question an expectant parent is asked? *"Are you hoping for a boy or a girl?"* And what is the typical response? *"It doesn't matter as long as my baby is healthy."* That seemingly innocent exchange may reveal a foundational belief that resides in the hearts of many of us—that there are few things worse for a parent than having a child who is not *healthy*. The possibility that we or someone we love would have a child with special needs evokes a powerful fear. Let's talk about that fear.

Who Are You?

We wish we were having this conversation at our kitchen table. We would love to hear your story before asking you to listen to ours. My wife Kris makes a great cup of coffee along with cinnamon rolls that are out of this world. Why not picture us communicating in that way? Our prayer is that this sounds less like an academic discussion and more like a chat between friends.

People generally pick up a minibook like this for a particular reason. What's yours? Perhaps you just learned that your child has some kind of mental or physical challenge. Maybe this diagnosis was made for one of your grandchildren or someone else for whom you care deeply. God may have brought such a special person into your church and you wonder about the best way to show love to the family.

Of course, this format does not allow us to hear what specifically motivated you to read this minibook. But, friend, God knows. Do you believe that? His Word goes so far as to make the outrageous claim that "the very hairs of your head are all numbered" (Matthew 10:30). Your story—past, present, and future—is not hidden from his compassionate gaze.

Who Are We?

The Lord has blessed Kris and me with three children, two of whom are adopted. Our adopted son Andrew is blind and has a number of other physical and mental challenges. In many ways he functions like a small child and will never be able to live on his own.

As of this writing, Andrew just turned eighteen years old. We are in the process of organizing our household to care for him as an adult.

A Learning Experience

We have no desire to sugarcoat our story. There are aspects of caring for Andrew that are hard every day. Physical and mental handicaps are the result of a world rocked by sin. But we have learned that *hard is not necessarily bad*. Our experience is that God can truly work all things together for good (Romans 8:28).

Two thousand years ago, Jesus gave this invitation:

"Come to Me, all you who are weary and heavy-laden, and I will give you rest. Take My yoke upon you and learn from Me, for I am gentle and humble in heart, and you will find rest for your souls. For My yoke is easy and My burden is light." (Matthew 11:28–30)

This great passage has given our family four foundational truths that have guided us as we have tried to raise Andrew in a way that honors our Lord.

1. Be Authentic about the Pain

God does not expect his people to wear a plastic smile over a broken heart. All parents have dreams and aspirations for their children. Thoughts of your child playing sports, getting married, having a family, and caring for you when you're old are all normal for any parent contemplating the birth of a child. Often those dreams are dashed when you learn of your child's diagnosis.

Your child may never be able to speak. His life span may be greatly diminished. She may never be able to return or show love. He may never play sports, climb a tree, read a book, or go out on a date.

Your child may require lifelong care. She may never be able to feed herself. He may never be able to use the restroom without assistance. Simple words like

"Mommy" and "Daddy" may never come out of your child's mouth.

Never. That is a hard word for any parent to hear. But it is the reality for many mothers and fathers who have been given the challenge and privilege of raising a special needs child.

Honestly Acknowledge the Weight of Your Load

In his invitation, Jesus spoke to people who were "weary and heavy-laden." He doesn't ignore the hardship and pain that come with living in a fallen world.

Caring for a special needs child can be exhausting. We have experienced that with a son who is blind. One of the first lessons we learned was that sleep makes absolutely no sense to Andrew. It is always dark in his world, so why not be up at two o'clock in the morning? He went for years and years without ever sleeping through the night. Ever.

Andrew also had great trouble learning to walk. Because he could not see, he was not motivated to get up to go somewhere or to get something. He never saw another child walk so he had no model to follow. Lifting his head that far off the ground was terrifying to him.

Andrew also has complicated sensory issues, especially in his feet. Even touching the ground with his feet was extremely painful. That meant that until Andrew was eight years old, he had to be carried or placed in a stroller or wheelchair every time he needed to be moved. There were plenty of days when one or both of us were weary and heavy-laden.

2. Cry Out to the Lord

What does a Christian do in such a situation? Ignore the pain because big boys don't cry? Wear a plastic smile? Just pretend everything is fine?

Approaches like that are not even close to what the Bible advocates, nor are they consistent with Jesus' invitation. God wants his people to genuinely and passionately cry out to him. Jesus says, "Come to me." He is urging us to bring our hurts, our questions, and even our complaints to his throne of grace.

One Scripture passage we treasure is Psalm 61:1–2: "Hear my cry, O God; give heed to my prayer. From the end of the earth I call to You when my heart is faint; lead me to the rock that is higher than I."

In his book *Soul Physicians*, biblical counselor Robert Kellemen writes about the importance of developing spiritual candor, which he defines as courageously telling oneself the truth about life, "in which I come face-to-face with the reality of external and internal suffering." He goes on to say, "In candor, I admit what is happening to me and I feel what is going on inside me."[1]

That is exactly right. Friend, please do not listen to anyone who says you have to be some sort of super-mom or superdad as you raise your special needs child. Syrupy Christianity that denies the reality of suffering in this life is unbiblical. It won't be able to sustain you through the challenges and hardships that lie ahead in this journey.

Do Not Be Afraid to Express Questions, Confusion, Doubt, or Complaint

Some people believe it is wrong to question God. Really? That is not the message of the Bible. For example, the prophet Habakkuk was very concerned and hurt about what he perceived as injustices all around him. So what did he do? He took his questions to the throne of God.

> How long, O LORD, will I call for help, and
> You will not hear?
> I cry out to you, "Violence!" yet You do not
> save.
> Why do you make me see iniquity, and
> cause me to look on wickedness?
> Yes, destruction and violence are before me;
> strife exists and contention arises.
> Therefore the law is ignored and justice is
> never upheld.

> For the wicked surround the righteous;
> therefore justice comes out perverted.
> (Habakkuk 1:2–4)

Those are the sounds of an authentic conversation between the Lord and one of his faithful servants. Commenting on Habakkuk's questions, one writer said

> God is the friend of the honest doubter who
> dares to talk to God rather than about him.
> Prayer that includes an element of questioning
> God may be a means of increasing one's
> faith. Expressing doubts and crying out about
> unfair situations in the universe show one's
> trust in God and one's confidence that God
> should and does have an answer to humanity's
> insoluble problems.[2]

The same is true of a man named Asaph. He wrote Psalm 73, one of the most important discussions of suffering in the entire Bible. We would encourage you to drink deeply from this psalm, which illustrates a man who came to God with questions and complaints. He did so respectfully—there is no question about that. But he admitted, with words that Jesus would later use himself, that he was weary and burdened because he had questions and challenges that were beyond his own wisdom and strength.

Understand That in So Doing, You Are Being Like Christ

Jesus not only gave this invitation, he also modeled this kind of emotional and spiritual authenticity. Do you remember the words Jesus uttered from the cross? "I am thirsty" (John 19:28). "My God, My God, why have You forsaken Me?" (Matthew 27:46). The same compassionate Savior who invited us to acknowledge situations that make us burdened and weary was willing to do the same thing himself in his hour of greatest need.

How about You?

Have you been willing to honestly acknowledge the weight of your situation? Have you come to understand that it is okay to cry as you consider the special needs of your child? Can you bring yourself to admit that you are burdened and weary? When you think about the way you have responded to this trial thus far, would the word *authentic* be an accurate description? If not, what needs to change in the way you talk to God and others about the difficulties you are facing?

3. Accept the Responsibility

Jesus not only encourages us to acknowledge our burdened, weary condition, he also urges us to do something about it. Using a word picture that everyone in that day would have understood, Christ invited men and women to "Come to Me. . . . Take My yoke upon you and learn from Me" (Matthew 11:28–29). John MacArthur helpfully explains this metaphor.

> A yoke was made of wood, hand-hewn to fit the neck and shoulders of the particular animal that was to wear it in order to prevent chafing. For obvious reasons, the term was widely used in the ancient world as a metaphor for submission. The yoke was part of the harness used to pull a cart, plow, or mill beam and was the means by which the animal's master kept it under control and guided it in useful work.[3]

Yes, It Is a Yoke

A yoke allows the wearer to accomplish something that is hard. Jesus practiced full disclosure when he explained that following him would involve this kind of submission to his plan.

Never Forget That It Is Jesus' Yoke

One of the most important words Jesus uttered that day to his potential followers was also one of the smallest: *my.* Every challenge we face is one that our Lord and Savior chose for us.

We remember the morning that Andrew's diagnosis was becoming clearer. We were at our state's Children's Hospital, and Andrew was connected to all sorts of monitors and machines. He was only a few weeks old, and we were not even sure if he would survive. Our hearts were filled with fear, doubt, hurt, and uncertainty. It felt like we were in the middle of a hurricane where we had no idea what was going to happen next. Our emotions were real and raw.

Looking back, we are thankful that God created us with the ability to feel pain in a way that is deep and rich. It felt like falling off a motorcycle at a high rate of speed and skidding down the highway while layers of skin are being peeled off. It exposed parts of our existence that normally went unseen. The volume was turned up on every aspect of our being in a way that only pain can do.

But we are also thankful that God has given us more than our emotions. As we felt deeply, we also tried to get our mental bearings by thinking biblically about what was occurring to us and in us. Eventually that led to a mental conversation that went something like this:

1. Is there anything about this situation that is outside of God's control? *No.*
2. Could God have prevented this from happening to Andrew and to us if he had chosen to? *Yes.*

3. Will God ever give us more than we can bear?
   No.
4. Can God use this situation for his glory and our
   good? *Yes.*
5. Has God promised to go with us as we try to raise
   our son for him? *Yes.*
6. Will we accept this responsibility and seek to
   joyfully submit to his plan for our family?
   Absolutely.

One of the reasons you can joyfully accept the yoke
of raising a special needs child is because the One who
has provided this opportunity is "gentle" and "humble
in heart" (Matthew 11:29). As the writer of Hebrews
would later explain, Jesus is our sympathetic high priest,
seated on a throne of grace (Hebrews 4:14–16). Any
yoke he places upon us will be placed with gentleness,
humility, and abundant grace.

It Will Never Be More Than You Can Bear

The Lord made an incredible promise through the
apostle Paul to his followers in Corinth.

> No temptation has overtaken you but such as
> is common to man; and God is faithful, who
> will not allow you be tempted beyond what
> you are able, but with the temptation will

provide the way of escape also, so that you will
be able to endure it. (1 Corinthians 10:13)

You may be reading this and wondering, in light
of your current challenges, how this promise could pos-
sibly be true. One answer may be that you can "endure
it" better if you allow others in your life to help. The
Scripture commands us to "bear one another's bur-
dens" (Galatians 6:2). Sometimes that means humbling
ourselves and being willing to receive help from others
in our family, church, and neighborhood. That is not
always easy for people who like to be independent and
self-sufficient. Yes, there is the legitimate concern that
no one else can care for your child as well as you can. But
one of the ways that Jesus' yoke is easy and light is that
he provides people to help us carry the load.

Balance the Weight of Your Yoke
with the Glory of Eternity

The responsibility Jesus has given us is only tempo-
rary. We realize that your response might be, "But didn't
you say that Andrew would never be able to care for
himself on his own?" Yes, our yoke is one that Jesus has
given us to bear for as long as we are on this earth. But
that is just a vapor compared to the length of eternity.
These first eighteen years of Andrew's life have gone by
at an incredibly brisk pace. He is now taller than his

mom and quickly gaining ground on his dad. It seems like only yesterday that we brought him home from the hospital to begin our journey.

God's Word frequently calls us to consider our challenges in light of eternity. Consider these delightful passages of Scripture:

> In this you greatly rejoice, even though now
> *for a little while,* if necessary, you have been
> distressed by various trials, so that the proof
> of your faith, being more precious than gold
> which is perishable, even though tested by
> fire, may be found to result in praise and glory
> and honor at the revelation of Jesus Christ;
> and though you have not seen Him, you love
> Him, and though you do not see Him now,
> but believe in Him, you greatly rejoice with
> joy inexpressible and full of glory, obtaining as
> the outcome of your faith the salvation of your
> souls. (1 Peter 1:6–9, emphasis added)

> Therefore we do not lose heart, but though
> our outer man is decaying, yet our inner man
> is being renewed day by day. For *momentary,*
> *light affliction* is producing for us an eternal
> weight of glory far beyond all comparison,
> while we look not at the things which are

seen, but at the things which are not seen; for the things which are seen are temporal, but the things which are not seen are eternal. (2 Corinthians 4:16–18, emphasis added)

How about You?

Have you ever told the Lord that you will joyfully accept his yoke? Has there been a definite time in your life when you acknowledged your sin and placed your faith in the death, burial, and resurrection of Christ as your only hope of salvation? Is Jesus your Lord, the One who is qualified to provide the perfect blend of blessings and trials to make you more like him (Romans 8:28–29)?

If not, why not take a moment to accept Jesus' invitation to take his yoke upon you?

4. Prepare for an Adventure

There will never be a person in heaven who regrets accepting Jesus' yoke of salvation and service. The Lord promises two great rewards for those who accept his invitation.

The Adventure of Learning

Jesus said that those who accepted his yoke could in turn "learn from Me." We would each say that having Andrew has been an incredibly rich learning opportunity.

For example, we have learned the power of the gospel. Scripture tells us we are united with Christ in his death, burial, and resurrection. We have come to understand the power and beauty of death. What do I mean by that? Andrew's challenges sometimes reveal the sinfulness of our own hearts. Andrew is not the only person in our family with *special needs*. When these sinful thoughts, desires, words, and actions surface in our own hearts and lives, we can choose to put them to death because of what Christ has already done for us. The privilege of parenting Andrew has revealed aspects of our hearts and lives that God wanted us to address.

Thankfully, it does not stop there, with death, because the central focus of the gospel is the empty tomb. Jesus is alive and we can therefore embrace the new life that is available in him. We are learning what Paul meant when he said, "do not go on presenting the members of your body to sin as instruments of unrighteousness; but present yourselves to God as those alive from the dead, and your members as instruments of righteousness to God" (Romans 6:13). If Jesus had given us an easier parenting assignment, we might not have been as motivated to take important steps of spiritual growth.

We have also learned about the sufficiency of God's Word. We are frequently out of answers. But we have come to recognize that this position of dependence can be a very good place. With the psalmist we say, "Before I was afflicted I went astray, but now I keep Your word"; and "It was good for me that I was afflicted, that I may learn Your statutes" (Psalm 119:67, 71).

Lastly, we have learned many lessons about God's sufficient grace. We feel very akin to the apostle Paul, who asked God to remove his "thorn in the flesh" three times (2 Corinthians 12:7). God's powerful and compassionate response was the following:

> "My grace is sufficient for you, for power is perfected in weakness." Most gladly, therefore, I will rather boast about my weaknesses, so that the power of Christ may dwell in me. Therefore I am well content with weaknesses, with insults, with distresses, with persecutions, with difficulties, for Christ's sake; for when I am weak, then I am strong. (2 Corinthians 12:9–10)

This is not a yoke we would have chosen for ourselves. But we can now be profoundly thankful that Jesus keeps his promises. Every yoke he offers includes opportunities to learn. We know more about ourselves and more about our Savior than we would have ever learned had this trial not been entrusted to us.

The Adventure of Divine Rest

Jesus promised that he would give rest to those willing to take his yoke. That concept was so important that it was mentioned twice in this brief interchange.

It is humorous for us to think about the word *rest* and the name *Andrew* in the same sentence. Honestly? The two do not go together very well. But when the Bible uses the word *rest*, it is often speaking about something other than physical sleep. "Rest for your soul" involves peace, comfort, and assurance that God will continue to sustain you as you abide in him.

Part of this is *the rest of contentment*. We are firmly convinced that caring for a special needs child is God's perfect will for us. There is a sense of peace and contentment that comes over you when you really believe that God has a plan for your life, and that his plan is good. "'For I know the plans that I have for you,' declares the LORD, 'plans for welfare and not for calamity to give you a future and a hope'" (Jeremiah 29:11).

There is also *the rest of joy*. We wish you could meet Andrew. We wish you could come to our house for an evening and listen to him laugh. Sure, he has special needs. But he also possesses a cluster of gifts and abilities that brings absolute delight to anyone he touches. There are times almost every day when Andrew says or does something that makes all of us break out in uproarious laughter.

Last is *the rest of fulfillment.* Several years ago a family from our community came to our church, completely unsolicited, and gave us 100 acres of beautiful property. It has many wonderful features, including a stocked fishing pond. That was a perfect gift for a family with a blind child. We have spent countless hours fishing together in the summertime.

One evening as the sun was going down Andrew asked if we could pray together so that he could trust Jesus as his Savior and Lord. We never wanted to force him to make that decision. We taught him the gospel, but we always wanted faith to be a decision he initiated. We wish you could have been there on the bank of that pond when our special needs son cried out to Jesus in repentance and faith. He took Jesus' yoke upon him and is now learning and growing in him. And the beautiful thing is, even though he has challenges and struggles that will never go away, Andrew too has found rest for his soul. Having that experience as a parent was one of the most fulfilling experiences ever. Thank God for giving us such a delightful yoke!

Endnotes

1. Robert W. Kellemen, *Soul Physicians* (Winona Lake, Ind.: BMH Books, 2007), 300.

2. Kenneth L. Barker and Waylon Bailey, *The New American Commentary,* vol. 20 (Nashville, Tenn.: Broadman & Holman, 1998), 277-8.

3. John MacArthur, *Matthew* (Chicago: Moody Press, 1989), 279.

Simple, Quick, Biblical

Advice on Complicated Counseling Issues for Pastors, Counselors, and Individuals

MINIBOOK

CATEGORIES

- Personal Change
- Marriage & Parenting
- Medical & Psychiatric Issues

- Women's Issues
- Singles
- Military

E YOURSELF | GIVE TO A FRIEND | DISPLAY IN YOUR CHURCH OR MINISTRY

New Growth Press

Go to **www.newgrowthpress.com** or call **336.378.7775** to purchase individual minibooks or the entire collection. Durable acrylic display stands are also available to house the minibook collection.